STUDENT HANDBOOK

My Personal Tapestry of Life (A Self Awareness Model)

Written by:

Dr. Barbara Thomas-Reddick

Print information available on the last page

Rev. date: 01/13/2016

To order additional copies of this book, contact:
Xlibris
1-888-795-4274
www.Xlibris.com
Orders@Xlibris.com

"Who Are You?"

Name

DEMOGRAPHIC

Hopefully by now, you have read Dr. Barbara Reddick's book, The Presence of a Chaplain & My Personal Tapestry of Life. If you have not, we encourage you to first read the book before moving forward with this handbook.

This section will allow you to take a look at self in order to become aware of who you are and who you may want to become. Please read each question carefully and explain in detail your thoughts, feelings, concerns and observations.

Please understand that this is your personal tapestry of life and only you will read it unless you decide to share as I have. The journey in this student handbook will hopefully allow you to become empowered with your self awareness. Work at your own pace, realizing that you can stop and start at anytime.

(If you feel uncomfortable answering any of the questions, move on to the next question until you complete it. At the end of the journey, you may feel comfortable to revisit the unanswered questions.)

NAME: _____

DATE: _____

TIME: _____

AGE: _____

EDUCATION

7th ◯   8th ◯   9th ◯   10th ◯   11th ◯   12th ◯   1yr college ◯   2yr college ◯   3yr college ◯
4yr college ◯   5yr college ◯   6yr college ◯

Male: _____
Female: _____

Please check how many children you have.

Children: 0-1_____   2-3_____   4-5_____   6-7_____   8-9_____   10 _____
◯ Married
◯ Divorce
◯ Single
◯ Dating
◯ Student

Share how you are feeling at this moment. (in detail)
_____
_____
_____
_____
_____
_____
_____
_____
_____
_____
_____

Do you have a clue of what you would like to learn about yourself?
YES _____   NO _____

Explain what you would like to learn about YOU?

What is your favorite food? _____

What is your favorite game you like to play? _____

Do you have a hobby? _____

Who is your favorite Artist? _____

What grade are you presently in? _____

Do you have a favorite sport? _____

If you could meet a celebrity, who would you choose? _____

WHO RAISED YOU?

Mother ○ Father ○ Grandma ○ Grandpa ○ Sister ○ Brother ○ Auntie ○ Other Family ○

Uncle ○ Pastor ○ Friends ○ Neighbors ○ Teacher ○ Cousin or Other ○

WHAT IS YOUR FAVORITE COLOR?

Do you have a pet, if so share the name?

_____

_____

_____

_____

If you have a pet, describe the level of care you provide for your pet.

_____

_____

_____

_____

How many pets have you had in your lifetime? _____

From a scale from 1 to 10, how would you number yourself as the level of care for pets? 1---don't care at all for pets   10--- care a whole lot

_____

Do you attend church? (do not have to answer)
YES _____   NO _____

If you attend church, temple, or synagogue? What is your denomination?

_____

_____

_____

What do you like about your church, temple, or synagogue?

_____

_____

_____

What would like to be when you grow up?

_____

_____

_____

How many siblings do you have? (circle)

1 ○ 2 ○ 3 ○ 4 ○ 5 ○ 6 ○ 7 ○ 8 ○ 9 ○ 10 ○

How many step sisters or step brothers do you have?

1○ 2○ 3○ 4○ 5○ 6○ 7○ 8○ 9○ 10○

Do you like school? If no, explain why.

_____
_____
_____
_____
_____
_____
_____
_____
_____
_____

If you like school, explain in detail what you like about school and why?

_____
_____
_____
_____
_____
_____
_____
_____
_____
_____
_____
_____

While growing up who raised you? Explain this experience.

_____
_____
_____
_____
_____
_____

_____

_____

_____

_____

_____

Are you okay with who raised you? If yes explain, if no explain.

_____

_____

_____

_____

_____

_____

_____

How was your upbringing? Explain

_____

_____

_____

_____

_____

_____

_____

_____

Paint the picture in words, how you would like for your family to look.

_____

_____

_____

_____

_____

_____

_____

_____

_____

_____

If you could change one thing about your family lifestyle, what would it be?

_____

_____

_____

_____

_____

What do you enjoy most about your family?

_____

_____

_____

_____

Are you being raised by both parents, single parent, or no parent, etc? Explain

_____

_____

_____

_____

_____

_____

_____

_____

Which parent do you feel comfortable to share your deep thoughts with? Mom _____ Dad ___ Other_____

Who is your favorite teacher and why?

_____
_____
_____
_____
_____
_____
_____
_____

What is it you like about this teacher?

_____
_____
_____
_____
_____
_____
_____
_____
_____

If you could change one thing in your school, what would it be?

_____
_____
_____
_____
_____
_____
_____
_____
_____

Do you like your school that you are presently attending?

_____

_____

_____

_____

_____

_____

_____

_____

_____

If yes, why, if no why?

YES: _____

_____

_____

NO: _____

_____

_____

While growing up, did you spend time with grandma and grandpa?

_____

_____

_____

_____

_____

_____

_____

_____

_____

If you spent time with either, explain how you felt then and now?

_____

_____

_____

_____

_____

If you did not spend time with grandparents, how do you feel about this?

_____

_____

_____

_____

_____

Do you feel that there are benefits for children who have grandparents in their lives? If so, why? If not, why?

_____

_____

_____

_____

_____

Make an observation of how you are feeling NOW.

_____

_____

_____

_____

_____

Do you feel that this student handbook is helping you thus far?
YES _____   NO _____

What do you enjoy doing when you have free time?

_____

_____

_____

What is your strengths?

_____

_____

_____

What is your weaknesses?

_____

_____

_____

If you could change one thing about you, what would it be and why?

_____

_____

_____

If there is something you could change, do you feel that this has hindered you from moving forward in your life?

_____

_____

_____

Do you feel that life haven't been fair?

YES _____   NO _____

EXPLAIN:

_____

_____

_____

_____

_____

_____

If you feel that life for you hasn't been fair, identify one thing you can do to move things forward in a positive manner.

_____

_____

_____

_____

_____

Name one thing that you really dislike for someone to say or do to you? Is there someone you are angry with?

_____

_____

_____

_____

_____

_____

If there is someone you are angry with, why?

_____

_____

_____

_____

_____

_____

Have you tried to resolve this matter?
YES _____   NO _____

Do you want to resolve the matter if it is not resolved at this time? If yes, how do you plan on putting this behind you?

ACTIVITY

TAKE TIME TO WRITE A LETTER TO SOME ONE YOU WANT TO MAKE AMENDS WITH!
THERE MAY BE MORE THAN ONE PERSON.
USING THE NEXT FORMAT or YOU CAN USE YOUR PAPER.

FROM: _____
_____
_____

TO: _____
_____
_____

Dear _____:

_____
_____
_____
_____
_____
_____
_____
_____
_____
_____
_____
_____
_____
_____
_____
_____
_____
_____
_____

Sincerely,
_____

TAKE A BREAK!!!!!!!
Debrief

Self Care

Embrace the moment of your true feelings and know that if you are feeling angry, mad, happy, sad, or some anxiety, it's okay.

Examples of taking a break:

a. Take a walk
b. Drink a cup of coffee or hot tea etc.
c. Deep Breaths
d. Self Care

WELCOME BACK!!!!!!

TAKE AN OBSERVATION OF HOW YOU ARE FEELING AT THIS TIME.

_____
_____
_____
_____
_____
_____
_____
_____
_____
_____
_____
_____
_____
_____
_____
_____
_____
_____
_____
_____
_____
_____
_____
_____

External and Internal Alterations

Have you ever used drugs?
Yes _____ No _____

Have you ever used alcohol?
Yes _____ No _____

If yes, what type of drug have you ever used?

If no, explain on a separate sheet of paper, sharing a moment in your life where you wanted to use but didn't.
_____
_____
_____
_____
_____

What kept you from using?
_____
_____
_____
_____
_____

Share this experience of how this make you feel that you were able to not use drugs or alcohol.
_____
_____
_____
_____
_____

Cannabis _____ Heroin _____ Cocaine _____ Crack Cocaine _____
Hallucinogen _____ Ecstasy _____ Methamphetamine _____
Molly _____ Flakka _____ Alcohol _____ Other_____

Please explain the age you started using drugs? _____

Who introduced drugs to you? _____

How do you feel about this person today?

_____
_____
_____
_____
_____
_____
_____
_____
_____

Did you trust this person at the time he or she introduced this drug to you?

_____
_____
_____
_____
_____
_____
_____
_____
_____
_____
_____

What would you do differently, if you could turn back the hands of time?

_____
_____
_____
_____
_____
_____
_____
_____
_____
_____

How do you feel about leaders?

_____
_____
_____
_____
_____
_____
_____

How do you feel a leader should lead?

_____
_____
_____
_____
_____
_____
_____
_____
_____

If you attend church, temple, or synagogue, how do you feel about your pastor, rabbi, or priest, etc.? Does your pastor, rabbi, priest, etc., exemplify good leadership skills?

_____
_____
_____
_____
_____
_____
_____
_____
_____

If not, identify the areas you would like for your leader to improve in.

_____
_____
_____
_____
_____
_____
_____
_____

Define leadership.

_____
_____
_____
_____
_____
_____
_____
_____
_____
_____

How do you feel about this overall observation of self and others?

_____
_____
_____
_____
_____
_____
_____
_____
_____

Would you recommend this workbook to someone else?
Yes _____ No _____

GREAT WORK!!! YOU DESERVE A PAT ON THE BACK. I look forward to speaking with you in the near future. We can arrange for a conference call, if you'd like.

Dr. Barbara Thomas-Reddick

WHEN YOU DO NOT KNOW WHO YOU ARE, YOU WILL BE WHAT OTHERS WANT YOU TO BE!!!

"WHO ARE YOU?"

WHEN YOU COMPLETE YOUR HANDBOOK, IN ORDER TO RECEIVE YOUR CERTIFICATE OF COMPLETION, CONTACT Dr. Barbara Thomas-Reddick at 850-559-4016 or email me at DrBarbaraReddick@gmail.com.

IF YOU WOULD LIKE TO BOOK DR. BARBARA REDDICK FOR FUTURE ENGAGEMENTS FEEL FREE TO CONTACT ME AT THE NUMBER ABOVE.

WEBSITE:
www.thepresenceofachaplain.com

Stay focused for upcoming book on PARENTING!

Printed in the United States
by Baker & Taylor Publisher Services